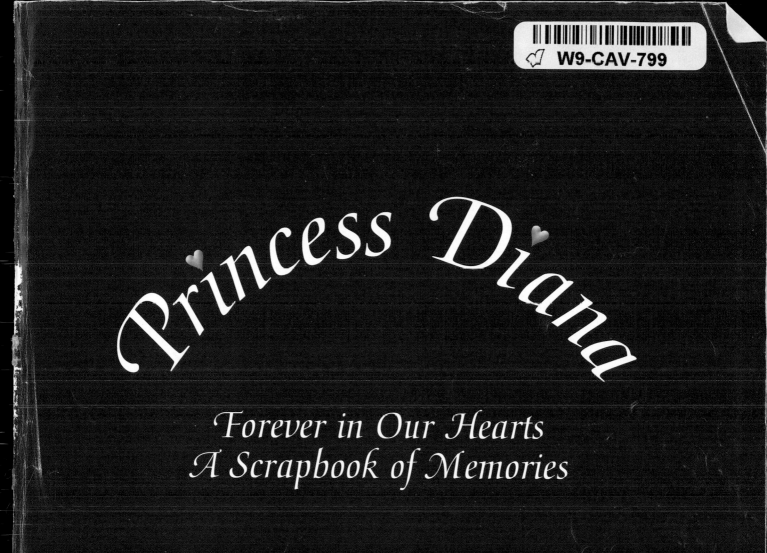

Princess Diana

Forever in Our Hearts
A Scrapbook of Memories

by Kimberly Weinberger

SCHOLASTIC INC.

New York   Toronto   London   Auckland   Sydney
New Delhi   Hong Kong   Mexico City

ISBN 0-439-04529-0

12 11 10 9 8 7 6 5 4 3   9/9 0 1 2 3/0

Printed in the U.S.A.
First Scholastic printing, November 1998

Introduction

Her life was the stuff of which fairy tales are made. With her beauty, her grace, and, most of all, her kindness, she brought great joy to her country and to the world. More than just a royal figure, she opened her heart to millions, earning their love and respect in return.

Her name was Diana, and this is her story.

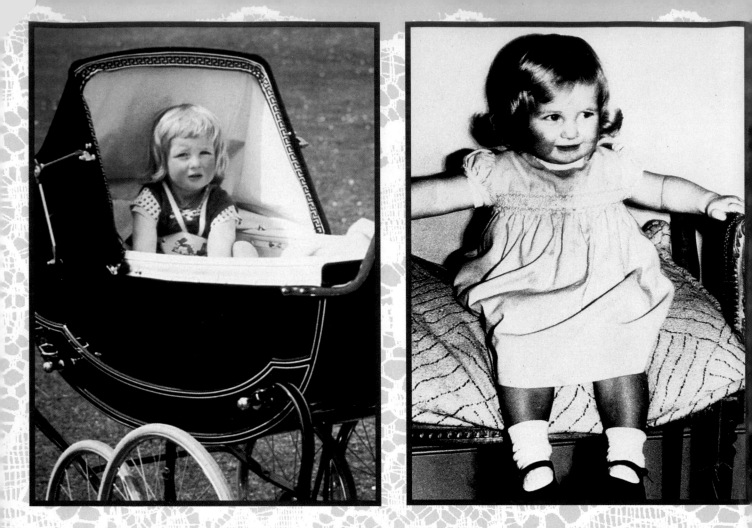

A Future Princess Is Born

On July 1, 1961, a baby girl was born to John and Frances Spencer. Already the parents of two daughters, the Spencers had hoped for a son. They took a week to think of a girl's name for their child!

Though they didn't know it at the time, the name the Spencers chose would one day be known around the world. Diana Frances Spencer was born to lead an extraordinary life. The Spencers lived on a beautiful estate called Park House, just next door to the country home of the Queen of England herself. Little Diana loved her home and spent much of her time playing outdoors. With scenic woods, stables for horses, and a heated swimming pool, Park House seemed a perfect setting for a future princess's early life.

Growing Up

Surrounded by woods filled with rabbits, fox, and deer, Diana developed a great love for animals. She happily fed and cleaned up after all kinds of pets, from hamsters to goldfish to her beloved guinea pig, Peanuts.

Three years after her birth, Diana's parents had a fourth child, a son. Diana was thrilled with her baby brother, Charles. The two became inseparable, spending countless hours together on their family's huge estate.

Diana's childhood was filled with changes. When she was just six years old, her mother moved out of their home. Diana and her sisters and brother grew up with nannies to care for them.

Though she was a polite, sweet child, Diana did not always like the women hired to look after her. She once threw a nanny's underwear on the roof, and she locked another in a bathroom!

Diana Cares for Children

Diana loved to care for others, especially young Charles. Whether sad, upset, or just lonely, Charles knew he could turn to his sister and she would always be there for him.

Her love for children led Diana to become a teacher's assistant. At age eighteen, she taught dance, drawing, and painting to kindergarten children. Diana also looked after the son of an American family living in England.

The Lady Meets Her Prince

Though she was barely aware of it growing up, Diana was actually a member of the nobility in England, holding the title Lady Diana. Because of this, she was acquainted with the royal family, which was headed by Queen Elizabeth II. The Queen's eldest son, Prince Charles, would one day be crowned King of England.

Diana's connection to the royal family earned her an invitation to Prince Charles's thirtieth birthday party. Hundreds were there, but Diana's beauty and shy smile caught the Prince's eye. Months later, Charles and Diana became a couple.

"Will You Marry Me?"

The news about Charles and Diana's love soon spread. The shy young teacher's aide quickly became famous. Everyone wanted to know if the Prince had finally found his Princess.

The answer came in February 1981. Prince Charles asked Lady Diana to be his wife. Blushing with happiness, Diana accepted. The fairy tale had begun—and Diana's life would never be the same.

Becoming a Princess

With the wedding less than six months away, Diana had a lot to learn about being a princess. She frequently visited Buckingham Palace, the magnificent London home of the Queen of England, her future mother-in-law. There, Diana's royal training began.

To practice walking down the aisle, Diana paraded through the palace with a sheet tied to her waist. She also had to learn to dress like a princess and to sit for hours while her portrait was painted.

By far the most difficult part of her royal education was the constant presence of the media. Quiet and shy in public situations, Diana could not get used to the cameras that followed her wherever she went. It was a problem that would plague her for the rest of her life.

The Royal Wedding

On July 29, 1981, more than 750 million people watched on television as Diana wed her Prince. A glass coach brought the bride to St. Paul's Cathedral. There, more than 2,600 guests awaited her arrival.

Her twenty-five-foot silk train trailing behind her, Diana walked down the aisle toward Charles. "You look wonderful," said the Prince. "Wonderful for you," Diana whispered.

After the ceremony, the happy couple drove past cheering crowds back to Buckingham Palace. They kissed on a balcony as thousands applauded below. It was a magical day for Diana and for the world.

Honeymoon at Sea

The Princess and her Prince followed their fairy tale wedding by sailing into the sunset. Diana and Charles cruised the Mediterranean Sea on the royal yacht, *Britannia*.

Of course, this was no ordinary honeymoon. Though they were the only guests on the ship, the couple had a crew of 276 officers waiting on their every need!

After the cruise, Charles and Diana continued their honeymoon at the royal family's Scottish estate, Balmoral Castle. Glowing with happiness (and a deep tan from the Mediterranean sun!), the Princess posed with her new husband and charmed photographers with her smile.

A Royal Welcome

Diana thought the public would soon lose interest in her. She couldn't have been more wrong! Four months after the wedding, a visit to Wales proved that the people loved their new Princess.

Thousands gathered in the rain to shake hands with Diana. Because the crowd was so large, the Prince and Princess had to split up to cover all of the people. When he greeted his part of the crowd, the Prince was met with groans. They wanted Diana! Still, Charles handled his reception with humor, apologizing for having only one wife!

Scenes like this were repeated again and again in cities around the world. Rain or shine, Diana was welcomed with open arms wherever she went.

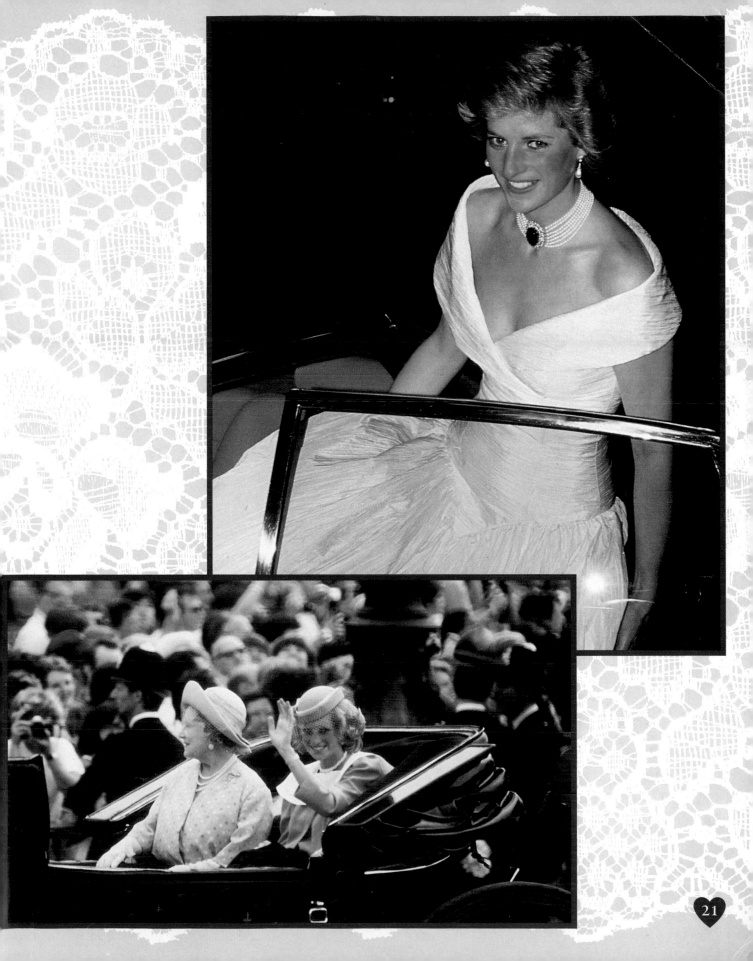

An Heir Is Born

On June 21, 1982, the young woman who loved children gave birth to a baby of her own. It was a boy, and England celebrated as Prince William Arthur Philip Louis was introduced to the world.

With his blond hair and bright blue eyes, it was obvious who William resembled. Queen Elizabeth confirmed this when she said of her grandson, "Thank goodness he hasn't got ears like his father!" As firstborn son and future king, little Prince William held an important place in the royal family. But Diana would not let her son's life be one of strict rules and "proper" behavior.

From the start, Princess Diana took control of her son's future. Though William would normally have been raised by nannies, Diana insisted on caring for him herself. "Wills" was her greatest joy.

The Birth of Prince Harry

Two years later, Princess Diana gave birth to another son. Prince Henry Charles Albert David arrived on September 15, 1984. The people called him "Harry." His father, Prince Charles, called him "absolutely marvelous."

Two-year-old William accompanied Charles to the hospital to visit his mother and new baby brother. Less than twenty-four hours later, Charles and Diana brought home the newest addition to their family, with the crowds (and the cameras) looking on.

The press trumpeted the news that Diana had given the royal family just what they wanted — "an heir and a spare." Little William, of course, was the heir who would one day be King. Harry, the spare, would rule only if his brother could not.

Diana and Her Boys

Protective and affectionate, Diana loved being a mother. She remembered the stories Charles had told her about his strict and often lonely childhood. Diana worked hard to help her boys through the difficulties of royal life.

From their first steps to their first days at school, Diana was there, encouraging her sons with the joy of a proud parent. Rather than hiring private tutors as was royal custom, she insisted that the boys attend school with their friends. When she and Charles traveled to foreign countries, they often took the Princes with them.

At nearly every major moment of their young lives, the world seemed to be watching William and Harry. Like their mother, they were destined to live in the spotlight.

Diana's Style

As her children grew, Diana blossomed. No longer shy and awkward, she had grown into her role as Princess. Diana brought a fresh new style to the usual fashions of the royal family.

Princess Diana's clothes were always big news. She had more than one hundred gowns, eighty suits, and countless dresses. If she wore a blue velvet gown to a party, copies of it were in stores the very next day!

When appearing with her husband, Diana always wore low-heeled shoes. The Prince and Princess were the same height—five feet ten inches—and Diana didn't want to tower over Charles.

The Way You Wear Your Hat ...

All women in the royal family must wear hats to formal daytime events. Though she had never worn anything more than a baseball cap before, Diana grew to love this custom. With her sense of style and fun, she made a statement with each hat in her huge collection.

Wearing everything from wide-brimmed creations to caps with feathers, the Princess stood out in any crowd. Even with her head uncovered, she made headlines. Diana's hairstyles received just as much attention as her hats.

Diana Reaches Out

Though her family was always her first priority, Princess Diana soon realized that she could use her royal position to help people. And so the Princess went to work.

Diana's travels often put her in touch with the sick and the poor. Her heart ached when she saw a hungry child or held the hand of an ill person. Princess Diana knew she could help, and she did.

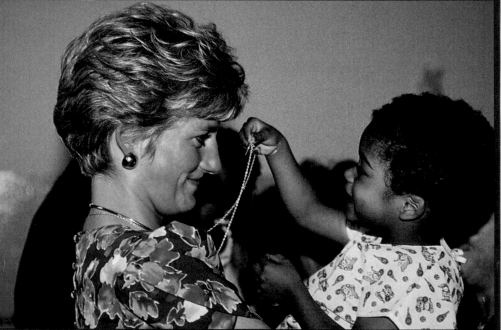

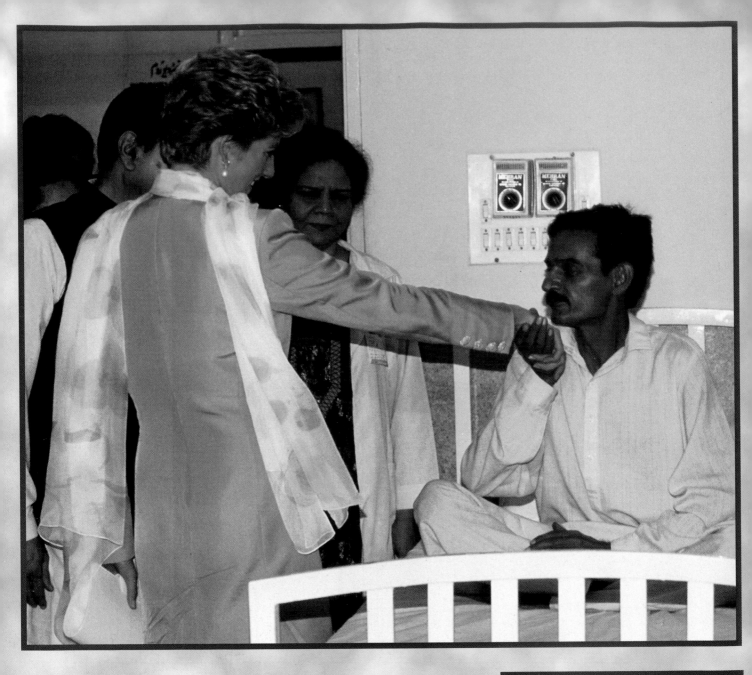

A Powerful Voice

When the Princess attended an event for charity, the amount of money raised doubled because she was there. Diana spoke out on everything from homelessness to drug addiction.

One issue close to her heart was AIDS. As the first royal to shake hands with a person suffering from this horrible disease, Diana made history — and spread hope.

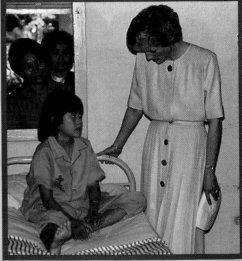

On the Go

As the years passed, Diana's work increased. At one point, she was president of twenty-seven charities! Though her schedule kept her busy, Diana tried to relax and stay fit by going to the gym, playing tennis, or swimming nearly every day.

It was at this time, too, that a new figure entered the royal family. Sarah Ferguson had fallen in love with Prince Andrew, younger brother to Prince Charles. In 1986, the couple married, and Diana gained a sister-in-law and close friend.

A Mother's Love

No amount of work could ever keep Princess Diana away from the two most important men in her life, William and Harry. Diana always had time for her sons.

From roller-coaster rides to white-water rafting, Diana tried to give her boys as normal a childhood as possible. But she also made sure they understood their royal responsibilities to help those less fortunate than themselves.

Sad Endings and New Beginnings

Though Diana's marriage had begun as a fairy tale, it did not end that way. Over the years, the Prince and Princess had grown further and further apart. On August 28, 1996, the royal marriage was officially over.

For Diana, the end of her marriage was also the start of a new life. The Princess continued her important work with a new confidence and an eye on the future.

The People's Princess

Princess Diana now knew she would never be Queen of England. But her hope was to become "queen of people's hearts" by helping others. In an interview, Diana said, "I think the biggest disease this world suffers from . . . is the disease of people feeling unloved. I can give love . . . and I'm very happy to do that. I want to do that."

Diana's independence seemed to give her a renewed passion for life. She continued her charity work with even greater conviction and also discovered new causes to support. Diana spoke out against the military's use of land mines, underground bombs that maim innocent people. Once again, her efforts brought the world's attention to an important but often ignored issue.

The Death of Diana

Diana's dreams of a happy ending would not come true. On August 30, 1997, news broke that stunned the world. Diana's car had crashed in a tunnel in Paris, France. The Princess was dead.

Millions sat glued to their televisions, unable to believe Diana was truly gone. In the days following her death, thousands of flowers and notes were left at the gates of Buckingham Palace. It seemed the entire world was weeping for its lost Princess.

Saying Good-bye

Diana's funeral took place on September 6, 1997. Nearly one million people stood in complete silence as her casket made its way through the streets of London. The sad clanging of the bell at Westminster Abbey was the only sound that could be heard.

Prince William and Prince Harry walked behind their mother's casket, along with their father, their grandfather, and Diana's brother, Charles. After the service, Diana was buried on her family's estate, Althorp.

The Queen of Hearts

Though the Princess of our modern-day fairy tale is gone, her spirit lives on. Most important, she lives in her two boys, William and Harry, who do their mother's memory proud as they grow up.

Diana is also honored in other ways. The Diana, Princess of Wales Memorial Fund, established shortly after her death, has raised millions of dollars for Diana's favorite charities. A memorial garden is also planned near her London home, and there are hopes to issue a British coin engraved with Diana's image.

This Princess touched the world with her spirit. She touched our lives with her humanity. Her name was Diana, and she will live in our hearts forever.